GOLDEN SOVEREIGNS

and some of lesser value

from Boadicea to Elizabeth II

GOLDEN SOVEREIGNS
and some of lesser value

from Boadicea to Elizabeth II

Nicolas Bentley

CHANCELLOR
PRESS

First published in Great Britain 1970 by
Mitchell Beazley Limited

This edition published 2003 by Chancellor Press,
an imprint of Bounty Books, a division of
Octopus Publishing Group Ltd,
2-4 Heron Quays, London E14 4JP

Designed by Wendy Bann

Printed and bound in Spain

ISBN 0 7537 0845 0

To Jolly Sir Roger

CONTENTS

INTRODUCTION

England is one of the few countries in the world that still has a monarchy. No one seems to know quite why this is. Looking back over our history at the various varlets, lily-livered loons, black sheep and eccentrics who have occupied the throne at one time or another, our affection for the institution of monarchy seems hard to understand. Nevertheless, the toast is still The Queen, God bless her and all who sail in her.

There have been exceptions, of course, in the long catalogue of our monarchical misfits – Alfred the Great, Edward the Pacemaker, Albert the Good, and George the Fifth. But these few are hardly enough to account for our belief that a king, or queen, is a good thing in him-, her-, or itself. And if exception be taken to Albert's inclusion among the kings, well, he may not have worn the crown, but he obviously wore the trousers, for when they came down in 1861, to be neatly folded and borne away by the Great Valet who keeps an eye upon all things, Victoria was as a lost sole swimming rudderless in a tank of tears, knowing not which way to proceed. As a result, she went sideways for a while, until headed in the right direction by Disraeli.

There is no doubt that in the modern state the institution of monarchy, with its court and courtiers and its elaborate protocol, so much more courtly, more protocular than the humdrum, homespun, drip-dry entourage of a common or garden president, is an anachronism. Not that drip-dry drips drip only in the corridors of presidential power. At the Court of St James's, for instance, one can think of – however, let us not digress. For the time being, we have got a nice clean queen in whom we can all take a pride. Moreover, she is *regnant.*

Very few of England's queens have counted for much, and fewer still have been regnant. Pregnant, yes; and some have been repugnant; some both repugnant and regnant; a few perhaps regnant, repugnant *and* pregnant. It is impossible to say with accuracy who were which or what or why because of history's tendency to bastardy. It is a fact, however, that there have only been seven queens regnant, not counting Henry VII. It is not known after which of these sovereigns Queen's Pudding was named – a mystery that offers grounds for amusing speculation.

The naming of queens is in itself something of a mystery. Who,

9

in his right mind, would call his daughter Cynethrith, the name of poor Offa's wife? And then there was Edward the Elder's wife, Eadgifu, and Edgar's Aethelflaed, her predecessor in his affections being known as Wulfthryth, by whom Edgar had a daughter, Eadgyth. And then all of a sudden Canute went and married a girl called Emma. William the Conqueror later on married Matilda, and Henry I, a spineless copy-cat, did exactly the same. And then there was Henry II's wife, an Eleanor. But after this came names like Mary and Elizabeth and Anne – terribly middle class. Nevertheless, the monarchy has somehow managed to preserve through all the vicissitudes through which it has shuffled, stumbled, skidded or shot along on its beam-ends, an aura that has surrounded the dignity and title of sovereign from the time of Alfred the Great to that of our own Farming Equipment and Allied Machinery Queen, crowned annually at Olympia amid the plaudits of a bucolic court.

It is difficult, because of the mists of time and so forth, to say who was actually the first King of England, but most authorities seem to plump for Boadicea. And this is strange when you come to think of it, because despite the well-known insularity of the British people, they have always shown a penchant for being ruled by foreigners. True, there has not yet been a Japanese King of England, nor an Israeli, but no doubt the future will take care of this, for in the past we have had monarchs who came from Scandinavia, France, Germany, Holland, among other countries. So Nicaragua, what's keeping you?

If it should seem superfluous in this supposedly democratic age to dwell upon the majesty, or the malevolence, of kings, let this work be read as history must be written – in order that we may understand how best to avoid repeating the mistakes of the past, such as William Rufus, Richard III, or George IV. In former times there was a tendency among biographers of royalty to temper criticism with a reverence for monarchy *per se*. Today, nurtured on authorities more sceptical, such as Lytton Strachey, Trevelyan and Godfrey Winn, we look upon royalty with a more searching gaze. It is the object of the present work to focus that gaze upon the subject even more closely, to illumine with the beam of perfect candour the characters and actions of those who have

10

held sway over the British people, whether by right of inheritance or by force of arms and legs, as in the case of Cromwell's jackboot athwart the neck of England's green and pleasant populace.

A word now about the royal features here reproduced. With the exception of Boadicea, whose likeness is based on a description by the later historian, Dio Cassius, all are founded on contemporary sources in the form of coins, medallions, busts, or portraits. I am indebted also to descriptions given in Mr Grant Uden's invaluable record of appearances, *They Looked Like This*.

I am grateful to my friend Bill Mitchell and to Mrs F. E. Dawkins for pointing out two ludicrous errors that occurred in the first edition. These have been rectified and I trust the book will now be found to be free of blemishes, except for the first four Georges.

BOADICEA
61 A.D.

In contrast with the turbulent lives and turbulent deaths to which English kings were often prone in the past, the lives of most English queens have been uneventful. Almost all of them have died in their beds – three double and three single, the odd queen out being Boadicea, or as it is now the fashion among the pedantry to call her, Boudicca, Queen of the Iceni, nowadays known as the East Anglians.

On the death of Boadicea's husband, Prasutagus, who reigned by kind permission of Nero and died without heir, the Romans seized his lands. This made Boadicea livid and, as *Time* would say, she feuded with the Romans for ages, until eventually they got fed up and scourged her. They also handed over her daughters to the common soldiery. And, of course, some soldiers *are* terribly common. I mean think of REME—

Well, this was more than flesh and blood could stand, even though Boadicea's allowance of both was well above the average. She roused the people of East Anglia, marched southward to Colchester, followed by a screaming rabble, downed a plate of oysters, and went into battle.

Tacitus in his *Annals* records that ere the fight was joined in Camulodunum, as Colchester then was, the Romans saw 'a fearful apparition . . . in the estuary of the Thames'. This, of course, cannot have been Boadicea because she was footing it from the opposite direction. The apparition must therefore be recorded as a UFO. Anyway, it put the fear of Gods into the Romans, who abandoned Camulodunum and tore westward, skidding to a stop near King's Cross. Here Boadicea eventually caught up with them and slogged it out with the Roman general Suetonius (naturally enough known among his troops as Suet Pud) until there was scarcely a Briton left. Preferring suicide to a fate worse than death, Boadicea took poison.

The Greek historian Dio Cassius, who lived about a century after Boadicea, when her fame and figure were already legendary, describes her as fierce and lofty, with a harsh voice and huge masses of fair hair. Those who remember Florence Austral as Brünhilde will be immediately struck by the resemblance. Those who saw the real thing must have been equally struck, especially if unwise enough to be standing near her chariot,

which had knives fixed to its wheels. These, rotating with their action, reduced her enemies, if not in numbers, at least in height.

A statue of Boadicea in her chariot, sweet and swinging low, stands on the Victoria Embankment at the corner of Westminster Bridge. It conveys admirably the proud independence of her spirit in showing her about to cut into the traffic at right angles to the main stream.

ALFRED
871-901

What went on between the death of Boadicea and the emergence on the scene of Alfred, nobody seems to have the faintest idea. One knows, of course, of the name of Edwin and about his dispute with Eadbald, or as he was affectionately called in the privacy of his daub-and-wattle residence, Bald 'ead, but apart from this all is more or less obscure. For a time, the land was ruled by squabbling gangs of Nordic nonenities, among whom the names of Hengist and Horsa ring a dim sort of bell. These were the Vikings, who lumbered about in the twilight of the Dark Ages wearing hats tastefully trimmed with cows' horns.

Not a great deal is known about Alfred himself. Even the date of his birth is speculative. Among the known facts are that he was born at Wantage, Berks, and that he had two brothers, Aethelbald and, believe it or not, Aethelbert. Their father on Alfred's side was Aethelwulf, and continuing in the same vein, Alfred, in 868, married Ealhswith, daughter of Aethelred Mucill.

A considerable part of Alfred's life was spent in combat, either with his father-in-law or against the Danes, whom he eventually defeated, having invented the British navy. He captured the Danish king, Guthrum, and forced him, but *forced* him, to become a Christian, for Christ's sake!

Alfred was also a writer and translator; you will, of course, remember his *Encheiridion* and *Wulker's Grundiss zur Gesch. der angelsachsischen Literatur 386-451.*

About the cakes, it turns out that this was a complete fabrication. The thing was, he was sitting in this woman's cottage, you see, and she said to him, 'Would you like a cup of mead, dear?' not knowing who he was, you see. And Alfred, quick as a flash, said, 'Oo lovely, that's just what I meed.' A pretty ripe jest for those days. Anyway, he laughed so much he fell off his three-legged stool onto the hearth, accidentally tipping a pan of scones onto the embers. And that's how it all started.

Anyway, the Danes, who were raging atheists, practically wiped out Christianity in Britain, so as soon as Alfred got the upper hand, the first thing he did was to start up the monasteries again; but there weren't enough monks to go round, so he had to import some from France. They arrived as keen as *moutarde*, but it was up-hill work, the people having rather got out of the habit of

15

praying and fasting. However, things gradually improved and by the time Alfred passed away – his deathday, like his birthday, is uncertain – everybody had become frightfully good.

Viewed in retrospect, and seeing what Alfred had to put up with – as if the Danes weren't enough, he was also up against the witenagemot *and* the British working carl – his achievements were pretty terrific. For which reason posterity has nicknamed him Alfred the Great. The name is also applied to the manager of England's team, Sir Alf Ramsay.

ODDS AND EDS
901-1016

After Alfred came some assorted oddments known as the seven Eds – Ed the Elder, Edmund, Edred, Edwy, Edgar, Ed the Martyr and Eddie Ironside. In between came Athelstan, and bringing up the rear Ethelred the Unsteady. Of all this lot the only two who really count are Athelstan, who was pretty well the first to boss the Scots as well as the English, and Ethelred, because he let the Danes get away with it and so paved the way for another foreigner to ascend the throne of England. Disgraceful.

CANUTE
1016-1035

With our fondness for having foreigners to reign over us, Canute was an ideal king. He hadn't a drop of English blood, being a pure-bred great Dane. For no apparent reason he suddenly left Denmark, of which his father, Forkbeard, was king, and together they took over England. Later, Canute was forcibly ejected, but came back again and made a job of it, knocking out Ed Ironside, son of Ethelred the Unsteady, who claimed to have a prior claim.

Anyway, Canute turned out to be highly efficient and soon got everything going with a swing. His trouble was that his court was full of half-wits, who were all ludicrously sycophantic. One day they actually said to him, 'Sire,' they said, 'you really are the *tops*. You're so great, so marvellous, that if you were to tell the tide to stop coming in, it would stop.' Well, Canute thought, 'Ho ho, if that's what you think —' So they took an armchair down to the beach and Canute sat in it and when the tide began to come in he said, 'Hold! Advance no further.' Of course, in five minutes the water was over the top of his boots and the courtiers just stood there, their faces like beetroot. Canute told them they were simply a bunch of yes-men, and then went home and changed his socks.

Contrary to a common fallacy, Canute was not the first true-blue British monarch. Some five hundred years before his reign Arthur might have been seen picking his way with stately tread among the slag-heaps of the Cornish tin mines around Tintagel, or seated squarely at his Round Table surrounded by Sir Galahad, Sir Lancelot, Sir Lancelot's two cousins, Lionel and Bohart, known collectively as Lionel Bart, Gawain, Eric, or Little by Little, and other very parfitt gentle knights.

After he had become King of England, Canute still went on being King of Denmark, and not only that, he beat the Scots and eventually their leader, Malcolm Muggeridge, was forced to acknowledge him as overlord. They never forgot it, and to this day it's not safe even to mention Canute's name in Sauchiehall Street.

HAROLD I
1035-1040

Harold I was an absolute bastard, by no means the only one to become King of England. He was the son of Canute and Aelgifu (one of the Northamptonshire Aelgifus). She was, poor woman, as you can well imagine, the victim of an oft-reiterated jest ('Aelgifu a thick ear if you don't watch it').

Despite his illegitimacy, Harold had the nerve to claim Canute's throne when Canute died, and in 1037 was actually elected king after objections by his half-brother, Hardicanute, and a re-count.

Harold was also known as Harefoot, on account of doing the mile in four minutes, pursued up Watling Street by Hardicanute. He died in 1040, with absolutely nothing to show for his period as K. of E. A poor show.

HARDICANUTE
1040-1042

Hardicanute was perfectly *frightful* – cruel, oppressive and hardly ever known to say a civil word. After Harold died, out of sheer bloody-mindedness, Hardicanute had him dug up and chucked into a fen. And when the good people of Worcestershire objected to paying an enormous *geld* for the upkeep of the fleet, he burnt down the whole of Worcester. He gave the Earl of Northumbria a safe-conduct (of course, the earl must have been half-saved to have accepted it) and then had him murdered.

Hardicanute died on 8 June 1042, amid loud applause.

EDWARD
THE CONFESSOR
1042-1066

Edward the Confessor was just too good to be true. He was unbearably saintly. By comparison, Billy Graham would seem to be steeped in vice. All this sanctity was rather surprising, seeing that he was a son of Ethelred the Unsteady.

Throughout the whole of his reign people were rushing about all over the country attacking each other. Earl Godwine was going for Robert of Jumièges; Leofric and Siward were going for Godwine; somebody called Eustace was fighting everybody within reach; Beorn was having a go at Sweyn ('Take *that*, you sweyn!'); and King Gruffyd (Welsh Nationalist) was fighting Harold. It never stopped.

And throughout the whole thing, there was Edward, as cool as a cucumber, down on his knees praying from morning till night; what for, no one knows, unless it was that he should be kept out of trouble. If so, it just shows the power of prayer.

What it was that he confessed remains a mystery. So far as is known, his life was utterly blameless. Like Wenceslas, a good king, but a bit of a bore, don't you think?

HAROLD II
-1066-

It is easy to dispose of Harold II because he reigned for less than a year. Before he came to the throne (and, for that matter, while he was on it) things were in a state of chaos that beggars description. Hoards of people were scrimmaging about all over the place, up and down the Welsh border and all over the southern counties. Matters must have been further complicated, for Harold at any rate, by the fact that his wife was named Ealdgyth and his mistress Eadgyth, though possibly to avoid mistakes she was known as Swan-neck, while Ealdgyth's nickname was Bird-brain.

Flitting in and out of all this confusion was Harold's brother Tostig, whom he eventually banished; an incident that gave rise to the well-known aria, *Tostig's Farewell*. But anti-climax was to follow. In 1066 Tostig turned up again with a Norwegian acquaintance called Hardrada. Harold raced up from the south coast where he was on holiday and engaged them both in battle at Stamford Bridge. The pitch was in perfect condition and Harold beat the visitors quite easily.

While he was in the changing room word came that William, Duke of Normandy, had arrived uninvited at Pevensey, so he rushed down again to the south coast. At Senlac there was a battle, the outcome of which was later immortalized in the poem that opens with the lines:

> I shot an arrow into the sky,
> It came to rest in Harold's eye.

And that is how William won the day and became the first French King of England.

WILLIAM
THE CONQUEROR
1066-1087

William the Conqueror's father, Robert, Duke of Normandy, was what is known in his native land as *un morceau d'un diable*. He was, in fact, nicknamed Robert the Devil, added to which he was a bastard. However, far from following in his father's footsteps, William was of temperate habits and earnest demeanour, poor fellow. Throughout the greater part of his reign he was, needless to say, embroiled in one fracas after another, if not with his cousin Guy, who absolutely loathed him, then with Geoffrey (Three Star) Martel, or a gentleman by the name of Sweyn Estrithson. Trouble with the English led to the well-known invasion of 1066 and the capture of Hastings, where all that now remains of French influence are a few words such as *café, boutique, modes,* etc., displayed in hideous neon lighting along the sea-front.

William had little time to spare for anything except fighting, but was nevertheless surprisingly keen on embroidery, which led him to produce the Bayeux Tapestry.

At a time when few could write, except in Latin, and only those who wrote could read, William, undeterred by this, ordered the compilation of that fascinating work, *The Guinness Book of Records*, known in those days as *Domesday Book*.

William was about the only king whose uterine brother became Archbishop of Canterbury. Known as Odo (de-o-doh), he was about the only Archbishop of Canterbury who became Earl of Kent, and probably the only Earl of Kent who died in Palermo. This he did on his way to take part in the First Crusade, and no doubt was thus spared the humiliation of being cleft to the chine by a Saracen battle-axe, and I don't mean the wife of Barkiarok, the Sultan of Baghdad.

William's wife was Matty, daughter of Stanley Baldwin, King of Flanders, whom he married despite the opposition of the Pope, who himself had designs on Matty, but was never able to transfer them. However, all was eventually forgiven and in gratitude William established an abbey at Caen where he was buried in 1087, having died shortly beforehand.

In 1562 some Huguenots, for want of better amusement, dug him up and scattered his bones all over the place, for which, of course, their own were scattered in return during the ever-popular massacre of St Bartholomew's Eve.

WILLIAM RUFUS
1087-1100

We need not waste much time on William Rufus, otherwise
William the Second, who himself had little time for others, being
by nature violently impatient and consequently a rotten ruler.
On 2 August 1100, while hunting in the New Forest, he was killed
by an arrow fired by one who wished to remain anonymous. A
stone marks the spot where this kindly deed was performed.

Words fail me to describe the bestial character of Rufus.
Concerning his appearance, historians are unanimous in their
testimony, though the only surviving portrait, on a threepenny
bit, gives a rather different impression. However, he is generally
described as very fat, with a bull-neck that dwindled into sloping
shoulders, and was awkward in his gait. His eyes were deep-set,
his features heavy and coarse, and his face suffused with a hectic
flush. He wore his hair as long as that of any Chelsea lay-about,
and he had a frantic stutter. He died, need it be said, unmarried,
unmourned, and without issue.

HENRY I
1100-1135

Henry I was born, for a nice change, on English soil. But like many an English king, he spent a lot more time abroad than at home and was always popping over to the Cotentin peninsula, which he owned. It was while he was coming back from one of these jaunts that the incident of the White Ship occurred. He wasn't actually on board, as luck would have it, having switched to another ship at the last moment; but his son and daughter were, with a mob of their friends. The whole thing was very unfortunate because everyone started toasting the captain and the crew, who themselves got as high as kites and eventually ran the ship on to some rocks, and the whole lot.of them were drowned. Henry became extremely depressed about this – it was one of his crack ships – and from then on was known as The King Who Never Smiled Again. There is, however, no real evidence to suggest that this was much of a change. He hadn't got a lot to smile about at the best of times, even though events during his reign were by the standards of the period relatively calm.

In character Henry is said to have been on the whole a wise and just ruler; and by the same token cruel and despotic. He had an enormous (illegitimate) family, one of whom, Bob, became a thorn in the well-padded side of Stainless Stephen, his father's successor.

It was public knowledge that Henry kept a huge retinue of mistresses and also a menagerie,.both of which were a constant source of speculation and amusement to his subjects. He died on 1 December 1135 and was buried in Reading, of all places.

STEPHEN
AND MATILDA
1135-1154

King Stephen reigned, and so did chaos, from 1135 to 1154, with a brief interregnum between 1141 and 1148, when everything was in a terrible state o' chassis.

The painful truth is that Stephen just wasn't up to it. He was perpetually at loggerheads with various cliques and harried day and night by his cousin Matilda, a thoroughly unpleasant woman who, just because she was an empress (the widow of an obscure Holy Roman emperor called, rather improbably, Henry) seemed to think she could fling her weight about in England. Admittedly, she was the daughter of Henry I, Stephen's uncle, but as she had married, as her second husband, Geoff Plantagenet, this as far as the clergy were concerned (and they really ran the whole shooting match) put her out of the running, Geoff being not only a Frenchman, but also heir to some foreign throne or other, and the clergy detested pluralism, except among themselves. Also. the fact that Matilda's mother was a nun didn't help matters, Monks could do (and did) more or less what they liked, but not with nuns, whose persons were considered inviolate. Stephen could have captured Matilda perfectly easily on several occasions, but forebore to do so and let her go on rampaging about, stirring up trouble all over the place and saying she was Queen.

Not that there wasn't trouble a-plenty without any assistance from Matilda. In the Midlands the Earl of Essex was ravaging, pillaging, foraging and generally making a nuisance of himself; in the north the Earl of Chester, without so much as a by-your-leave, was carving out a principality for himself; and in the west the so-called Angevin crowd were having themselves a ball.

Well, eventually even Matilda got sick of it all. She decided to call it a day and went stalking back to France, leaving Stephen to get on with it. But Stephen's trouble was that he never got on with anybody for long, and when a few years later Matilda's son, Henry of Anjou, turned up and started making more trouble, he found ready support in various quarters.

At this stage Stephen said, 'I give up,' and agreed that when he died the throne should go to Henry. Well, of course, Henry couldn't *wait* when he heard this, and as a matter of fact he didn't have to for very long: Stephen died the next year and *voilà* – Henry was King!

HENRY II
1154-1189

It is to Henry II that we owe two distinctive and much-prized features of English life: (a) the jury system, (b) T. S. Eliot. It was Henry who really laid the foundations of the English legal system. In particular, he introduced trial by jury, the merits of which depend on whether you view the matter from inside or outside Wormwood Scrubs.

It was owing to Henry's sounding off in a moment of vexation that Thomas à Becket was sent prematurely to meet his maker, hence *Murder in the Cathedral*. Henry and Thomas were tremendous pals to start with, then Thomas began to get a bit too big for his chasuble and Henry, hearing of this, said something slightly indiscreet, which being overheard and misunderstood by some of his barons, resulted in their posting off to Canterbury and perforating Thomas, with fatal effects. Henry was fearfully upset when he heard this and knelt for hours at Thomas's tomb in his underclothes to show his remorse.

Note of ecclesiastical interest: among Henry's illegitimate progeny was one Geoffrey, the only bastard on record as having become an archbishop.

RICHARD I
1189-1199

From the word go, Richard was at it with broadsword, battle-axe or mace. He loved nothing better than a real set-to and spent most of his time hacking away at this adversary or that until struck down by a bolt from a cross-bow. He was, of course, known as Coeur de Lion, though to his intimates as Coeur d'Artichaut, from his having introduced the Jerusalem artichoke into England after a trip to the Holy Land, where with sword and Bible he laid about him, swatting Jews and Arabs alike as though they were black beetles; which, of course, is how he regarded them.

Naturally, being of such an antagonistic disposition, he made many enemies, by one of whom, Leopold of Austria, he was captured on the way home from a Crusade. As he lay languishing in a filthy Viennese jail, he heard outside his window the strains of *The Merry Widow*, and, peering out between the bars, saw Blondin serenading him on a tightrope. After a few weeks Leopold released him and Richard returned to England. But not for long. Soon afterwards he dashed over to France to have a go at King Philip Augustus and on 3 July 1194 knocked him flat and went on his way rejoicing.

As well as being a fighter, Richard was a friend of poets and troubadours. In fact, he was a bit of a poet himself. However, only fragments of his *oeuvre* survive, of which this is a fragment, written during the seige of Acre:

> While I applaud
> The dicta of Our Lord,
> The dicta of Mahomet
> Makes me vomit.

Richard married, in 1191, Señorita Berengaria, daughter of Sancho Panza, by whom he had, posthumously, a Cistercian monastery.

JOHN
1199-1216

It is impossible to find a good word to say for King John. Several bad words come easily to mind, but their use would involve the banning of this work by Messrs W. H. Smith. However, it may be said that he was rude, ill-tempered, obstinate, stupid, cruel, quarrelsome, tyrannical, selfish, bad-mannered, lax, sybaritic (and probably syphilytic too), oppressive, dishonest, crude, devious, cynical, a liar, a coward, a braggart, a degenerate, a bully, and a fool. He was also not to be trusted, and while his brother Richard was king, and was away in the Middle East, causing wholesale slaughter among the pagan populations, in the name of Our Lord Jesus Christ, amen, John tried to usurp the throne. Nevertheless, Richard later forgave him and named him as his successor.

When he came to the throne, John grew worse than ever, adding vices of the most disgusting (though albeit not unenjoyable) kind to the catalogue of his sins.

Well, of course, things couldn't go on like this, and eventually the barons went down to Maidenhead one afternoon, got hold of the King and pushed him into a marquee at Runnymede, and made him sign Magna Carta. This guaranteed the man in the street immunity from various forms of autocratic bloody-mindedness, but unfortunately said nothing about the powers of the trades unions, nor about the iniquity of the closed shop or the imbecility of demarcation disputes.

John, of course, was furious. He ground his teeth, swore, groaned and bit his nails before consenting to affix his sign manual to the fatal parchment. But as he hadn't got any alternative, he eventually did so, 'snarling with disappointed rage'.

His death on 19 October 1216 was an event for which Englishmen have ever since been thankful.

HENRY III
1216-1272

Henry III was a bit of a twister, partly no doubt because of the circumstances of his accession, at which time, for some unaccountable reason, large tracts of England were in the hands of Louis VIII of France. This, of course, was extremely undesirable, and was made even more so by some dastardly barons giving Louis their support. So it wasn't a very good start, particularly for a king aged nine.

Thereafter Henry's reign followed the familiar pattern: rows with the peerage, civil war, intrigues, etc., etc., with the high-minded Simon de Montfort stalking about and generally making things uncomfortable.

In 1255 the Pope, in what must charitably be assumed to have been a fit of aberration, suddenly offered Henry the throne of Sicily. Henry said thank you very much, but would *il Papa* mind, as he'd got a throne of his own, if he handed it on to his son? Henry's son, incidentally, was a round-shouldered child of ten, popularly known as Eddie Crouchback. The Pope said not at all, best of luck, and so little Eddie took the job on. Well, eventually the Mafia made things so disagreeable that Edward decided to swap the throne for the somewhat less glamorous but safer office of Count Palatine of Champagne and Brie, which, as he was apt to remark, was as good as a meal in itself.

The best thing about Henry III is Westminster Abbey, which he built and where he was buried, not a moment too soon for the fulfilment of his loving son's ambition to become king.

EDWARD I
1272-1307

We have Edward I to blame for the emergence of Welsh nationalism. It was his persecution of Llewelyn ab Gruffyd, look you, and his invasion of the land of Llewelyn's fathers that sparked the whole thing off, you see. As one man the Welsh arose – the Lloyds, the Georges, the Lloyd Georges, the Lloyd-Joneses, the Armstrong-Joneses, Owen Glendower, Morgan the Organ, Emlyn the Williams, Barry Parry, John Thomas, Taffy Thomas, the Pryses, the Rhyses, Rees Mogg, Mavis Davies and Edith Evans – as one man they rose, singing at the tops of their voices, and struck back.

Other notable trouble spots during Edward's reign were England, Scotland, Gascony, Sicily and the Middle East, where the filthy infidel was resisting every effort to bash him into a Christian frame of mind.

In 1290 Edward took it into his head to expel all Jews from England, bringing the catering and clothing trades virtually to a full stop. A few years later he nipped over to France for a spot of fighting and in his absence the Scots wha hae wi' Wallace bled and he had to rush back again to try and stop the rot. But by now he was getting on in years and instead the rot stopped him. He was buried in Westminster Abbey, where a plain slab commemorating this plain slab is inscribed with the well-known words, *'Edwardus primus Scottorum malleus hic est. Pactum serva in your old kit-bag and smile, smile, smile.'*

EDWARD II
1307-1327

You know the story about Edward, born at Caernarvon Castle, being held up, dribbling, by his Da in front of the people of Wales and proclaimed as their native prince, to the indifference of the handful of Owens, Joneses and Morgans who were hanging about? Not a word of truth in it. In fact, for some unaccountable reason the declaration was made at Lincoln, where the number of Welshmen per head of the local population is minute. Wherefore the Prince was later nicknamed the Lincolnshire Handicap, for so he turned out to be. In other words, a total loss, interested only in his boy friend, Piers Gaveston. Having no aptitude for the business of government, and little for anything else, he was only too pleased when a rather interfering friend of the family called Hugh le Despenser offered to take over as general manager.

The Scots, to whom the cardinal sin was (and is) frivolity, naturally detested Edward, who spent his entire time fooling about. At one period he thought it might be rather fun to have a go at relieving Stirling Castle, then under seige by 'Spider' Bruce, so he got together a raggle-taggle army and they all went up to Scotland, although it was only June. Well, finally he came face to face with Bruce at a place called Bannockburn, and aptly named too, because although Edward was not actually incinerated, he was certainly made to look like a bannock, i.e. a flattened oat cake.

Edward's end was undignified. Not only was he pushed off the throne by his barons, but his wife ran off with one of them. Afterwards he was shunted about from castle to castle until in 1327 he passed away.

EDWARD III
1327-1377

The reign of Edward III was enlivened by a number of interesting events, among them the Black Prince, the Black Death, the Battle of Crécy and the founding of the Order of the Garter. This came about quite by accident. Edward was strolling one day with Kent, Bohun, Burgh, March and Mortimer, chatting about the Statutes of Provisors and Praemunire, over which they were having a good laugh, when all of a sudden Edward's tights came down, causing even louder laughter. He decided there and then to institute the Order of the Garter, little thinking how strange a spectacle would be presented by some of its members clad in full Garter rig in the twentieth century.

Edward had two obsessions: one was chivalry, the other a belief that he was King of France as well as of England. No one quite liked to contradict him, except the French, who emphasized their disagreement with battle-axe and boiling oil.

When not engaged in trying to persuade the French of their error, as it seemed to him, Edward spent all his time and a considerable amount of Crown revenue on getting up tourneys and generally propagating the concept of chivalry, despite which he was a bit of a one for the damozels. He was, however, tremendously courtly and none footed it more featly than he when stately measures were trod. He also loved minstrelsie and gave much encouragement to lute groups. He died, a dotard, on 23 June 1377, leaving it to Kent, Bohun, Burgh, et al., to fight it out among themselves.

RICHARD II
1377-1399

Richard II was born at Bordeaux. It was natural therefore that his enemies should have referred to him when in his cups as château bottled. He was a son of the Black Prince, but apartheid had not yet reared its ugly head, and nor had Dr Vorster, so it didn't matter.

When he was only three Richard was brought to England, so that by the time he became king, at the age of ten, he had got used to English ways and to such quaint English customs as the levying of a poll tax – in this case fourpence per bonce or eightpence on Siamese twins.

Feelings ran pretty high about the inequality of the tax, which made no allowance for size, skin-heads being taxed at the same rate as big 'eads. Trouble inevitably followed, but little Dickey, who had taken to being king with as much relish as a student takes to pot, handled the situation with admirable calm.

One day, while he was sitting on his throne, he heard a schemozzle going on outside, and on enquiring what was afoot was told that it was the Peasants' Revolt. So this little lad – he was only fourteen, mark you – trotted off down the Mile End Road (then as now a place much resorted to by the peasants) and quashed the whole thing. However, the next day at Smithfield, the Lord Mayor, setting an extremely bad example for a man in his position, stuck a knife into Wat Tyler, one of the most revolting of the peasants. For a while it looked as though the whole thing might start up again, but lo and behold, young Dick stepped boldly forth and told them all to pack it in, and they did.

Unfortunately, after this promising beginning he didn't do quite so well. By dismissing Arundel, whom Parliament in its wisdom (excuse the contradiction in terms) had appointed as one of his chief ministers, Richard incurred the wrath of various MPs. And a wrathful MP in those days was not the sort of yapping pomeranian that we know now. He could bite as well as bark. Richard exacerbated MPs' feelings by increasing the power and position of one Michael de la Pole, a pal of his whom he elevated in the peerage, thus giving rise to the expression 'up the pole'.

In 1383 Richard married a girl called Anne of Bohemia (remember *The Bohemian Girl*?) but alas, she died in 1394,

causing him to become unhinged, if one may judge from the fact that two years afterwards he proposed to a girl of seven, Isabella, daughter of the Emperor of France, whom he eventually married, in spite of parliamentary opposition. As a matter of fact, Richard was used to parliamentary opposition. In 1386 Parliament had decided to take a tough line with him and Tricky Dickey had been forced to promise that he would play according to the rules. Eventually, however, he got so fed up with having to be answerable to Parliament for the exercise of his slightest whim that he declared publicly that the laws of England were in his mouth, not Parliament's. Nor did he stop at this. He next took to murdering his relatives, a policy that was bound to give offence, even though, having regard to the relatives in question, this would seem to have been a sensible move. He had Gloucester smothered, and Arundel beheaded. The Archbishop of Canterbury, with the respect due to his gaiters, was merely exiled.

Having continued to make away with those he didn't like, or who didn't like him, partly on account of his extravagance – he was always giving the most terrific parties – or because you never knew where you were with him, he playing cup-and-ball with you one day and his gaolers playing 'heads, bodies and legs' with yours the next – having continued successfully with this policy of elimination, he now embarked on a period of absolute monarchy, a nice change after absolute chaos. Feeling fairly confident that he had got everything buttoned up, locked up or locked out, he went over to spend a few days with some friends in Ireland. Fortunately, the Reverend Ian Paisley had not yet arrived on the scene, so Richard could still hear himself speak. But while he was away a cousin of his, Henry of Bolingbroke, got together with some friends who were disgruntled with the King and as soon as Richard got home, bingo – he was in the Tower!

To the surprise of all, the King – one up to him – said he couldn't care less. He admitted in writing to having behaved like an absolute shower, and then, if you please, read the statement aloud to the Press, thus confirming the suspicions of insanity aroused in 1396.

He spent the rest of his days in enforced retirement at

Pontefract Castle in Yorkshire, where in 1400 he died of a chill, and according to Shakespeare was also murdered. In the matter of his burial, too, you have a choice: he was interred at Kings Langley in Hertfordshire, or if you prefer it, Westminster Abbey.

HENRY IV
1399-1413

On the face of it, it would seem that Henry IV had absolutely no right to be king. His father, a person called Lancaster (not even one of the Lancaster Gates) had a few drops of the blood royal trickling through his veins, but his mother, also called Lancaster (they were first cousins, so small wonder that Henry wasn't particularly bright) had even less blue blood coursing through her arteries. Lancaster was the fourth son of dear old Edward III, but preferred for some reason or other to call himself John of Gaunt (deriving from the English attempt to pronounce Ghent, where he was born).

As a matter of fact, Henry came to the throne 'not so much by title of blood' (Capgrave), but because someone had the bright idea of *electing* a king, and Henry being the only candidate, he got the job.

Needless to say, his reign from start to finish was filled with strife and turmoil, to which he contributed not a little himself by conspiring with various clerical types and others, and then ratting on them when it suited his purpose. At one time, he had some idea of going on a Crusade, but very sensibly had second thoughts about it and went off instead to Lithuania (not much better) and got taken on by the Teutonic Knights (words and music by Ivor Novello).

Various well-known Shakespearean characters trip in and out of Harry's life story, among them Harry Hotspur, Mortimer Wheeler, Archbishop Scrope and Owen Glendower, better known as Owain ab Gruffyd, of Glendyyffvrddywyy, all of whom Henry either slew or defeated in preference to their doing the same by him.

For some reason best known to himself, Henry discarded the fashionable headgear of the day, the stockinette tam o' shanter with scalloped border, in favour of an embroidered tablecloth.

HENRY V
1413-1422

Henry V reigned for nine swinging years. Apart from his being rather too much given to prayer, he wasn't a bad sort. In fact, never a dull moment with Hal at the helm. Schism in the Church, war with France, political disturbances at home, rollicking in the Boar's Head, frolicking in a whore's bed, he was a right tearaway, was Henry – *and* he started the Hundred Years War. Agincourt was, of course, his high spot. This was the occasion on which in full view of the French he stiffened his sinews, summoned up his blood and lent his eye a terrible aspect, at the same time setting the teeth, stretching the nostril wide, holding the breath and bearing up his spirit to its full height. How he did all this and managed simultaneously to imitate the action of a tiger, we do not know. What we do know is that the French were so embarrassed at seeing him make such an exhibition of himself that they tiptoed silently away, leaving Henry in possession of the field.

HENRY VI
1422-1461

Henry VI had the unique distinction of ascending the throne at the age of nine months. While still a baby he appeared in Parliament, where his behaviour compared favourably with the conduct of a good many present-day MPs.

A few weeks after his accession he found himself also in possession of the throne of France. Later on this led to difficulties with the well-known spiritualist, horsewoman and transvestite, Joan of Arc, whose relatives later accused Henry of arson.

At home he had not only to contend with endless rows between members of his family and of his entourage, but with rabble-rousing Jack Cade, known as the Fair Maid of Kent, as well as with the Wars of the Roses. That he eventually went dotty is hardly surprising.

He is chiefly remembered as the founder of Eton, and his name is consequently reviled by many a juvenile member of the aristocracy.

EDWARD IV
1461-1483

The thing about Edward IV's reign was, you see, that at first
Warwick was perfectly friendly, but then got fearfully upset
because Edward decided to marry Liz Woodville instead of this
French girl, you see, that Warwick wanted him to marry; so
after that they were perpetually at odds (with the Nevilles and
the Pembrokes sneaking about in the background), Edward, of
course, being cheered on by Rivers and Salisbury, and Warwick
in league with Clarence, who loathed Gloucester, who naturally
supported Edward, who by this time, being flat broke, was forced
to ask Burgundy to lend him a fiver, which he did, thus saving
Edward's bacon. What little time Edward could spare from
matters of state and kidney pudding, of which he could never
have enough, he spent in the arms either of Jane Shore or Caxton.

EDWARD V
-1483-

Edward V is better known, curiously enough, as one of the Princes in the Tower. He wasn't known as either for very long because his uncle Richard is said to have taken against him and had the hapless youth and his brother Dick smothered with a pillow at the age of thirteen. When one thinks what some of the youths of today are like, and how seldom their uncles do us the favour of smothering *them*, it does seem a bit unfair.

RICHARD III
1483-1485

Richard III, better known as Laurence Olivier, came to the throne as a result of having done to death his nephew, Edward V, and stayed there as a result of his murdering (a) Henry VI, (b) Lord Hastings, (c) Lord Rivers, (d) Edward, Prince of Wales, and (e) Edward's brother Richard, the pair of them familiar to posterity as pathetic waifs in black velvet lounging about in the Tower of London.

Having thus eliminated all competition, Richard egged on the few friends he still had left to take part in a put-up job and offer him the crown, which, after a sickening pretence of modesty and surprise, he seized and stuck on his head.

The ins and outs of what went on before this, you simply would not believe. Honestly, the political and dynastic complexities of Richard's career are sheer murder. He began life in quite humble circumstances. His people were respectable north country folk (father, the Duke of York, mother, Cicely Neville, daughter of the Earl of Westmorland), who could hardly have guessed that one day their little boy would become King of England. However, to start with he was just a well-born youth and then for some reason or other he was made Duke of Gloucester. He was known, on account of his suffering from a spinal curvature, as Crookback Dick; also, on account of his reputation, as Dirty Dick, and because of his treachery as Dick Swiveller.

In the end his treachery availed him nought. Late one August afternoon in 1485, Henry Tudor, a sort of relative of Richard's, got absolutely furious with him and there was a battle between them at Bosworth in Leicestershire, near the A5. Richard, throwing to the winds such dignity as he possessed, ran about screaming for a horse and promising his kingdom to anyone who would furnish him with a nag. But there were no takers. Eventually Henry T. caught up with him and ran him through. As poor old Dirty Dick sank groaning to the sod, his crown fell off and rolled onto the grass. Whereupon some interfering little Lancastrian scuttled forward, picked it up and jammed it down on Henry's sweating brow, thus raising him from a mere peer to being the King of England; which in fact he had as little claim to be as Richard.

HENRY VII
1485-1509

The reign of Henry VII was chiefly notable for his bringing to an end that celebrated *bataille des fleurs* known as the Wars of the Roses and thus ensuring peace in England for at least half an hour. This he did by the simple expedient of marriage, paradoxically so often a cause of strife. He took for his queen, Elizabeth, daughter of Edward IV, thus uniting the houses of York and Lancaster.

Two curious things cropped up during Henry's reign. One was called Lambert Simnel and the other Perkin Warbeck. Simnel, who claimed to be the Earl of Warwick, in the hope that in some mysterious way this would entitle him to the succession, got involved with P. Warbeck, who also seemed to think he had some sort of claim to the throne. In fact, the nearest that either of them got to sitting on it was occupying a grace-and-favour dungeon in the Tower of London, whence P. Warbeck made bad his escape, being hanged after failing in the attempt. Simnel survived and spent his later years as a scullion, or as we should say, an *au pair* girl.

Henry VII, contrary to appearances, was no fool. He not only pacified those who so passionately proclaimed the virtues of *Gloria Vanderbilt* over those of the deliciously scented *alba Regalis*, but defeated a Scottish attempt at invasion (this was before the Rugby League provided an annual excuse for such events) and managed to stay on fairly friendly terms with the Irish; no mean feat, seeing how difficult it seems to be for the Irish to stay on friendly terms even with themselves.

It was one of Henry's rare parliaments that established the Star Chamber. This silver-gilt article was presented annually to the Minstrel of the Year at the Savoy Hotel, which was built by Henry.

By various means Henry managed in the course of years to accumulate a vast amount of money and thus became much disliked, except by the few who profited from his largesse.

HENRY VIII
1509-1547

As is well known, Henry VIII was terribly good at tennis, if not perhaps quite up to Wimbledon standards. He excelled not only on the tennis court, but was, in fact, a good all-round athlete, his all-round measurements being in the neighbourhood of 50 (topside) by 63 (fair round belly with good capon lined), 60 backside.

Henry, in addition to other accomplishments, possessed the gift of tongues and could utter the most frightful obscenities in several languages. Besides being an excellent linguist, he was a poet, a scholar, and a musician. Not only did he compose a number of dainty pieces, he also played the flageolet, tambour, tambourine, theorbo, rebec, citole, double curtall, descant and, if his audience was at this point still awake, the mandora.

In appearance Henry was decidedly impressive. One was immediately struck not merely by his height and girth, but by the size of his features, which were miniscule, in relation to the size of his face, which was enormous.

Even in an age of ostentation, Henry's taste in clothing veered towards the *outré*, and though such gear might nowadays pass unnoticed in the Chelsea Drug Store, there were not lacking those in his own day who thought the King's silks and satins, velvets and taffetas, plumes and furs, pearls and golden ornaments *just* a little bit on the showy side.

The King's manner, except when he was vexed by some awkward or idiotic prelate or irritated by some puling spouse, was genial and extrovert and won for him the nickname of Bluff King Hal. He was also known, from the ruthlessness of his disposition, as Hal Capone, and for other reasons as the Randy Dandy.

A notable high-spot in Henry's career was the Field of the Cloth of Gold, a sumptuous entertainment got up for diplomatic reasons by his opposite number across the Channel, François Iier. Its objective was undying harmony and friendship between their peoples. Its result was thirty-eight years of uninterrupted war.

The field itself was near Guînes, not far from Calais, and as soon as Henry was off the boat and through the customs, he went straight there, eager to embrace his future enemy. Having

travelled light he had with him a retinue of only 4,000. Catherine, his momentary spouse, had in her train a mere 1,200.

The party went on for three weeks, and so did the hangover from which many of the guests suffered. Wine was drunk in fabulous amounts and more than 2,500 animals were slaughtered to provide the all-singing, all-dancing assembly with food. Henry took his turn in the lists and knocked his opponent silly, then, being the kind of chap who never knows when to stop, went on to challenge Francis to a spot of wrestling. Unfortunately, Francis, with a full-Nelson, followed by a punishing head-lock and a swift cross-buttock, had Henry pinned to the canvas, arse upwards, in less time than it takes to tell. Henry was not unnaturally livid and this ignominious result more or less brought the proceedings to a close.

Henry was not at first much interested in politics, then he came under the baleful influence of Cardinal Wolsey, the inventor of combinations, who supported the King in his desire to get rid of his first wife, Katherine of Aragon, and marry Anne Boleyn. Had Wolsey survived, which fortunately he didn't, he would no doubt have supported Henry in his desire to get rid of Anne Boleyn and marry Jane Seymour, and to get rid of Jane Seymour and marry Anne of Cleves, and to get rid of Anne of Cleves and marry Catherine Howard. But Wolsey fell from grace, a donkey on which he was riding to Leicester Abbey, and died there on 30 November 1530.

Left to his own devices, which were extremely complicated owing to religious, dynastic, political and other factors, Henry got a bit above himself and started telling the Pope where to get off. The Pope rather resented this and there was a row. Unfortunately for His Holiness he had been having to contend for a long while with Martin Luther. And anyone contending with Martin Luther had also to contend with his world-famous constipation, which made him even more difficult to deal with than if he had been just an epileptic bigot. Henry, as a matter of fact, had supported His Holiness in his feud with Luther, and the Pope, in return, had granted him the title of Defender of the Faith, little thinking that 'ere long the cross to which Henry professed his attachment would become a double-cross. However, to cut a long story short, Henry suddenly shut down all the English monastries, thereby giving rise to our old friend the Church of England and causing hordes of unemployed monks to besiege the Labour Exchanges. This, of course, resulted in further trouble for the King, but he was not called Bluff King Hal for nothing. He bluffed his way out of this one by cooking a number of recalcitrant bishops in public. He also showed an iron hand beneath his velvet glove, trimmed with sequins and gilt *passementeries*, in dealing with the wily Welsh, the ignorant Irish, the fractious French, and a number of people living in the Isle of Wight.

In the end, worn out by his exertions in every direction, Henry died. The wonder is that he survived as long as he did, seeing the strain he put on his constitution and the strain the constitution, such as it then was, put on him.

EDWARD VI
1547-1553

One does not wish to speak ill of the dead, especially of a child, but it does look as though the English were let off lightly by the decease of Edward VI, who at the age of *thirteen* had read, with every sign of enjoyment, Aristotle's *Ethics* and was hard at it translating Cicero's *De Philosophia*.

In the few years left to this studious lad he showed himself, I regret to say, a worthy companion to his elder sister, who was to become known as Bloody Mary, displaying utter indifference at the execution of a pair of uncles whose lives he might easily have spared had he bothered to lift his little snub nose from the pages of Ovid's *Metamorphoses*. But no, in him the rheum of antiquity was thicker than blood. Mourned by next to none, this unhappy youth passed away in his sixteenth year.

LADY JANE GREY
-1553-

It was the fate of Lady Jane to have greatness thrust upon her. She found its weight insupportable and keeled over in a dead faint. This is absolutely true; it happened on 6 July 1553, after the death of Edward VI, when she was told she had got to be queen. She was only sixteen at the time and she flatly refused. But eventually she was talked into it and was proclaimed to all and sundry. Nevertheless, to this day some say she wasn't queen because she was never crowned. Anyway, Lady Jane's great-aunt Mary, affectionately known as Bloody, thought she had a better claim to the throne than her niece and was not going to stand being put upon; so after nine days of everybody shouting contradictory advice, Lady Jane was clapped into the Tower.

Without a shred of justification she was charged with high treason and being absolutely at a loss about what was going on, she pleaded guilty. Of course, her aunt shouldn't have done it, but what with being surrounded by a crew of fanatical and self-seeking RCs (and being an RC herself) and Lady Jane being C. of E., and everyone behaving as though they were stark staring mad, which some of them were, she gave in and signed Lady Jane's death warrant, and on 12 February 1554 the poor little doll had her head chopped off. End of chapter.

MARY I
1553-1558

Mary Tudor was unlucky from the start: her father was Henry
VIII and her god-father Cardinal Wolsey. She didn't make matters
any better for herself by showing distinct signs at an early age of
becoming a blue-stocking. At four and a half she could play the
virginals and at nine she could write in Latin and had begun to
learn Spanish, Italian and French. It was in English, however,
and in no uncertain terms, that she said what she thought about
those who had affianced her, without her leave, to the Dauphin
of France. Her displeasure is scarcely to be wondered at, as she
had never set eyes on him and was only two at the time.

However, the threat didn't last long. At five she was engaged
again – to her cousin the Emperor Charles V. But this didn't last
long either. Plans were soon afoot, believe it or not, to pair her off
with the Dauphin's *father*. But from this fate she also had a lucky
escape. Instead, the old man married her cousin's sister, thus
becoming Mary's cousin several times removed, though, as she
was wont to observe, not far enough.

Owing to the matrimonial machinations of her father, she had a
pretty thin time of it as a girl. Not only was she stripped of the
rank and title of princess, but also declared by her loving parent
to be illegitimate, and when she refused to acknowledge this soft
impeachment, was packed off to live at Hatfield. And don't
forget that in those days Hatfield was virtually a desert – no chain-
stores, no supermarkets, no petrol stations, no cinema, no bingo,
and the main street, instead of being jammed with cars all day,
was bone empty. It was enough to send the poor girl off her head,
and so it did.

Definite signs of mental strain began to set in, accompanied by
dizzy spells, shortness of breath, flatulence, hiccups and a general
feeling of lassitude. There was unfortunately little she could do
about this, except to try eye of newt, and toe of frog, wool of bat,
and tongue of dog, adder's fork, and blindworm's sting, lizard's
leg, and howlet's wing; none of which, contrary to the general
enthusiasm for such possets, did her any good. So eventually
she decided to pack it in and agree with her father that the Pope
was a dope and that she was what he said she was, although she
knew she wasn't.

Thus peace and harmony were restored *pro tem*. But on the

78

MARIA
REGINA
15+54

King's death and the accession, already described, of the well-known cat's-paw, Edward VI, a horrible little boy only nine years old, Mary's troubles began again.

Eddy was a noddy and did little or nothing as he grew up to alleviate the persecution of his step-sister, which was renewed with vigour by the gang of scheming gits who surrounded him day and night.

At the age of sixteen Edward performed the one judicious act of his reign. He passed away, throwing the court, aye, and indeed the nation, into utter turmoil. However, after a brief interregnum or nine days' wonder, known as the era of Lady Jane Grey, Mary came out on top and ere long became the bride of a dashing young *caballero*, Philip of Spain. A trifling difference of some thirty-one years in their ages was of no account compared with the importance of Mary's youthful spouse being a full-blown Roman Catholic, and in next to no time the Church of England was in the dog-house and Rome once more supreme.

Needless to say, the old guard didn't go for this at all and protested vigorously, but to no avail. Wholesale combustion of the clergy followed and Latimer, Ridley and Cranmer, old Archbishop Hooper and all, were soon burning merrily in the market place, along with others of their ilk to the number of three hundred. Thus did Bloody Mary demonstrate to one and all that she was a truly devout Christian.

She died, beloved of her people – with certain reservations among a few surreptitious Nonconformists – and fortified by the wrongs of the Holy Church.

ELIZABETH I
1558-1603

Queen Elizabeth was known for some reason or other as the Virgin Queen; a sobriquet that no doubt caused a quiet exchange of smiles between milords Leicester and Essex, not to mention Tommy Seymour, the Duke of Somerset's brother, and handsome Kit Hatton.

Elizabeth's reign was naturally a period of furious religious controversy. She, however, being something of a sceptic, steered clear as often as she could of the more exuberant manifestations of the Christian ethic, such as the stake, the rack, the thumbscrew, and so forth. She couldn't, of course, avoid such controversies altogether, being queen, though exactly *why* she was queen is something of a mystery. To start with, there was a good deal of speculation about her legitimacy and the gerrymandering that went on to make sure that she and no one else got the nomination was nobody's business. Certainly it was not her own, for at this period Elizabeth was used to doing what she was told, even when this meant going to live at Hatfield for a bit with her half-sister Mary, a whey-faced woman who couldn't stand the sight of her and was close on forty before she managed to get a husband and then had to make do with a Spaniard.

As a respite from this gloomy existence, Elizabeth was eventually packed off to spend a couple of months in the Tower, whence, to everyone's astonishment, not least her own, she presently emerged with her head not in her shopping basket, but still on her shoulders.

That Elizabeth survived these ordeals without ill effects shows that there was a strong streak of determination in her character. This was later to become apparent to some of her advisers when their aims clashed with her own. As she declared at Tilbury on the eve of the Armada, 'I know that I have but the body of a weak and feeble woman, but where there's a will there's a way. England expects this day that every man will do his duty, so up, Guards, and at 'em!'

Well, this was greeted with tremendous cheers and put new heart into everyone, except those who were about to have theirs cut out, along with their entrails, for venturing to disagree with the Establishment on the religious issue.

The Elizabethan age was not only the golden age of Eng. Lit., with Shakespeare, Jonson, Otway, Marlow, Kyd, *et al.*, tossing off masterpieces as easily as you might quaff a posset of ale; it was also a pretty lively period for Eng. Mus., with Tallis, Byrd, Morley and others then at the top of the charts producing madrigals, threnodys, galliards, pavanes, sarabandes, etc., for every sort of combination, e.g. trio (rebeck, viola da gamba, flageolet), quartet (rebeck, viola da gamba, flageolet, hautboy), quintet (shawm, rebeck, viola da gamba, flageolet, hautboy) and solo tambour.

In appearance Elizabeth was the living image of Dame Edith Sitwell, and like her was given to wearing elaborate clothes and fanciful geegaws. She was also given to swearing, spitting, picking her teeth in public, and dancing, her favourite measure being a *pas seul*, in which she was able to indulge those exhibitionist tendencies so abhorrent to the self-effacing disciples of that censorious Scottish homunculus John Knox, of whom it was said:

> John Knox
> Liked his whuskey on the rocks.
> He regarded gin
> As the unforgiveable sin.

Elizabeth led a charmed life. At a time when fame so often carried with it the penalty of the block, the rack, the poignard in the pancreas, or the interminable conversation of Lord Burghley, she survived to a ripe old age and died without hair on 21 March 1603.

JAMES I
1603-1625

The reign of James I is famous chiefly for the failure of that admirable enterprise known as the Gunpowder Plot. As usual, death and destruction were planned as a means of propagating the gospel of Christian love. Guy Fawkes, being an ardent convert to the Roman Catholic faith, regarded any other as blasphemy. James at the time of the plot was C. of E., but his religious affiliations were inclined to fluctuate. He married his daughter off to a Low Church *kraut* and would have married his son Charles to the Catholic Infanta of Spain, only the Spaniards weren't having any. And then he complained that people thought him cynical and an opportunist. He never cared much for politics; what he really wanted to be was a writer, but that he would ever have become a best-seller seems doubtful, judging from the title of his first effort, *Essayes of a Pretense in the Divine Art of Poesie*.

In appearance James was somewhat unfortunate, being squat, slovenly and bottle-nosed. Nor was his dignity added to by his habit of wearing a hat hugely tall and trimmed with ostrich feathers. Also he spoke with a Glasgow accent, which I suppose is all right if you're King of Scotland, as he was, but it definitely did not go down well with the English upper classes. However, as he was King of England as well they had to pretend not to notice.

CHARLES I
1625-1649

Charles I was a weak king; also a turncoat and a spendthrift; add to this a penchant for wearing lace collars and the picture becomes decidedly sinister.

In 1625 Charles married Henrietta Maria, daughter of the King of France. It was a sort of mixed marriage, she being an RC and Charles nominally Church of England, though with occasional reservations. Throughout his reign the Christian religion was, as usual, a cause of acrimony and violence. Archbishop Laud, under whose thumb Charles was, insisted on such things as the wearing of surplices and communion tables being placed at the *east* end of the church. Well, it takes no great feat of imagination to realize with what horror such devilish devices were regarded, especially in Scotland, where devilish devices have always been a fruitful and enjoyable source of friction.

Charles's reign was full of historical incident, e.g. the Star Chamber, which caused a lot of Prots to become Presbs; the Grand Remonstrance, of which, despite its grandeur, the King took not the slightest notice; and the business of Pym, Hampden and whatnot.

The King's part-time support of Anglicanism – at various times he was warm for various denominations – was only one cause of his being perpetually at loggerheads with Parliament, of which many loggerheads were themselves members. Another reason was his frightful extravagance, which at one time caused him to try and sell the Crown Jewels, but the idea fell through because he couldn't find a buyer, and in those days no one would have had the nerve to suggest the thing could be arranged if the King would agree to a 15 per cent rake-off.

Many of Charles's difficulties arose because of his chronic insolvency, and the only way he could get Parliament to vote him the money he needed, even for essentials, such as war with Spain or helping Protestant Danes to go and bash the Catholics in Germany, was to do Parliament's bidding. But as a dyed-in-the-wool autocrat with an exaggerated sense of divine mission, such a course was repugnant to Charles. However, he eventually had to bow the knee to its yoke and eat humble pie with a long spoon. He agreed to release various gentry whom he had imprisoned on a whim of the moment. The unkindest cut of all was the Commons'

insistence on his dismissing Buckingham, for long his *eminence grise*, or as some said, greasy. But at this point Charles put his foot down – as luck would have it, in a metaphorical cow-pat. He was desperate for money, but instead of dismissing Buckingham, he dismissed Parliament instead, so he was no better off.

A year later Parliament reassembled and the Commons started discussing things like tonnage and poundage, a fascinating if somewhat obscure subject, the mere mention of which was to Charles for some reason or other like a red rag to a bull. He immediately ordered the House to adjourn. The Speaker, a man of straw, tried to obey the injunction, but amid cat-calls, laughter, ironical cheers and cries of 'Sit down!' 'Shut up!' 'Shut up yourself!' 'Yes, we have no bananas!' and 'Does your mother know you're out?' was held down in the chair, kicking and screaming. (It later transpired that he was exceptionally ticklish.)

Such colourful scenes have disappeared, alas, from parliament-ary life and all we now get are bogus displays of spleen, readily dismissed afterwards by both sides as they down their gins and tonics at the bar.

For eleven years Charles ruled alone, except for the dubious advice of Laud, a nasty little piece of work with a passion for secular power and the outward evidences of Anglicanism, but little regard for the more ordinary of Christian virtues. His baleful influence on Charles met with what some might see as a just reward in his being beheaded.

Eventually the King's conduct led to the well-known Civil War, which was followed by the Great Plague, known as Oliver Cromwell. After a considerable amount of skirmishing, much of it in the Oxford area, to the irritation of various dons, to whom the study of the works of Diogenes, Socrates, Thucydides and Themistocles was of greater moment than the survival of consti-tutional government or civil liberties, Charles was captured. Eventually he was brought to London and tried, but as he had been improperly charged and neither judge nor jury was present, the unfairness of the whole thing did much to rehabilitate Charles in the affections of the populace, whose traditional sense of fair play, to this day strongly manifest at soccer matches, was outraged by the high-handed activities of Charles's opponents. The verdict having been decided upon before the proceedings began, Charles was condemned to death. His last word, uttered on the scaffold to Archbishop Juxon, was, 'Remember.' Unfortunately, he forgot to say what it was that Juxon was to remember.

OLIVER
CROMWELL
1653-1658

Between Charles's death and Cromwell's assumption of power four years later, there was no one to run the outfit; so Cromwell, taking a leaf out of Charles's book, ran it more or less himself. He was, in effect, the only English king never to be crowned, though many people, Charles especially, would like to have crowned him. He suffered from a deep sense of sin and is consequently acclaimed by members of the Lord's Day Observance Society as their patron sinner.

As is well known, Cromwell was a Roundhead, but he was also a square, hence his suspicion of anything unorthodox, such as Prince Rupert of the Rhine. In battle, Cromwell armed himself with a sword and a Bible, so that if he missed with one he could bore his opponent to death by reading aloud Ezra II, 43, or Luke III, 23.

Cromwell is generally credited with being the real founder of the British army. Someone who doesn't agree is Lord Montgomery. At the battle of Winceby (1643), Cromwell's horse was killed under him, a stroke of luck in a way: had he been sheltering from the battle on all fours, he might have been killed under his horse.

Many of Cromwell's sayings have remained famous to this day, such as 'Put your trust in God and keep your powder dry,' (addressed to his wife titivating herself in the bathroom), and 'Remove this bauble!' a reference to the presence of Charles I; also 'I had rather have a plain russet-coated Capstan that knows what he fights for and loves what he knows what he loves and what he fights for and why he fights whoever he fights for what he loves than knows not what he loves or fights for.'

In appearance Cromwell was somewhat unprepossessing, his best feature being a wart. His son Richard, who briefly inherited (1658-59) whatever it was that Cromwell sat on in place of a throne, didn't have a wart: he *was* a wart.

CHARLES II
1660-1685

Charles II, as is well known, was merry, but not until 1659, when he heard of the death of Cromwell.

During the Civil War he had lived abroad in reduced circumstances. Then in 1650, having arrived in Scotland and there been crowned king, he marched in triumph with his Cavaliers to Worcester, when Cromwell chased him up a tree. This the King thought to be an oak, till he discovered it was a gum tree. Whereupon he climbed down and made tracks speedily for France.

Following the news of Cromwell's death, Charles returned to England, home and beauty in the shape of Lucy Walter, Lady Castlemaine, the Duchess of Portsmouth, Catherine Pegg, Lady Shannon, Mary Davis, and of course, Nellie Gwyn, who between them produced eleven offspring sired by the merry monarch, who couldn't stop laughing. Another cause of merriment, apart from *Pilgrim's Progress*, was the visage of Titus Oates protruding from the pillory and adorned with a *maquillage* of flour, soot, eggs and tomatoes.

Besides being a patron of the tarts, Charles was an enthusiastic amateur scientist. He invented the King Charles spaniel and the Royal Society and was keenly interested in contraception. In fact, his last words were, 'Don't let poor Nellie calve.'

JAMES II
1685-1688

It was a piece of luck for James that he became King of England, because in fact he lived in France and was a simple *poilu* to begin with, and so not really in the running. However, at the time of the Restoration, which brought his brother Charles to the fore, restoratives were applied to him as well; so he quit the French army, joined the British navy as an admiral, and when Charles passed away, was piped aboard the throne.

James was a madly keen Catholic, which of course was strictly not allowed if you were king, but he utterly ignored this and naturally wanted all the disabilities that were imposed on Papists to be removed. For instance, no Catholics could hold public office and they were therefore debarred from being inspectors of weights and measures, House of Commons waitresses, or, of course, public lavatory attendants. James's advocacy of the cause of those who had set their hearts on inspecting weights and measures, serving tea and biscuits to MPs, or passing their days in the monastic seclusion of a public lavatory, so infuriated various bishops and others, that they got in touch secretly with James's son-in-law, a scheming Dutchman called Willie, and invited him over. The mere sight of his sly Dutch face and the sound of his guttural Dutch utterance were enough for James, who anyway hated his Dutch guts. He packed it in and went back to live in France, and that was that.

WILLIAMANMARY
1689-1694-1702

Mary, the female section of this conjugation, was the daughter of James II. Her better, or worse, half, according to your view of history, was an Orange. (She, of course, was a Stuart.) For five tempestuous years, beloved of her people, by whom she was affectionately known as the Half-Sovereign, she shared the throne with the Orange.

Following their marriage, they went to live at his place, which was in Holland, where she found things rather flat after the bustle and gaiety of London. However, as a dutiful wife and mother, as she would have been if she had had the chance, she soon adapted her ways to those of her new kith and before long the Orange was referring to her as 'my old Dutch'.

On the death of her dear old father, whom she couldn't stand, she returned to England. So delighted was she to escape from the stadtholders, margraves, burgermeisters, burgermistresses, meistersingers and bulb-fanciers of old Amsterdam – and who could blame her, except the Dutch? – that she seemed to take on a new radiance. This was said to be magically enhanced by the frequent absences of the Orange, who spent considerable time abroad interfering in other people's politics.

His fondness for doing this was first apparent in England, when he unexpectedly turned up one afternoon at Torquay, to the astonishment of those sitting in the Palm Court of the Imperial, and announced that he was going to occupy half the throne.

On another occasion he organized the well-known and popular massacre at Glencoe – being a strong believer in sassenach supremacy, and a Dutchman to boot – for which he was ever afterwards known north of the border as the Blood Orange.

While he was away in foreign parts, Mary governed the country more or less single-handed, and when the occasion demanded it, showed herself capable of firmness. Her actions now and then were not without a touch of humour, as when she imprisoned her uncle, the Earl of Clarendon, for some sort of treason, thereby endearing herself warmly to his countess.

In character Mary was said to be pious, charitable and subdued, a combination sufficient to explain the Orange's frequent trips abroad. She died of the fashionable pox on 28 December 1694. The Orange, who survived her by eight years, was pipped on 8 March 1702.

ANNE
1702-1714

There is not a great deal to be said about Queen Anne. It is generally agreed that she is dead. While living, she was both fat and inordinately greedy, the one being a natural consequence of the other, and she also liked a drop of the hard stuff. She was deeply religious and with true Christian charity loathed everyone who did not belong to the Church of England. She governed the country to the best of her ability, and so did the Duchess of Marlborough.

The duchess was for several years the Queen's closest friend. In fact, so intimate did they become that all formality between them was dropped, the Queen calling the duchess Mrs Freeman and being called Mrs Morley in return. This was regarded in some circles as tantamount to democracy and going a good deal too far, and when, after a quarrel, the duchess was given the push, there were not lacking those who said, bridling and in tones of disapproval: 'Yes, well, you see, I mean, well, yes, well it's all very well, isn't it, eh?' However, the Queen, who could take a fiercely independent line over matters that didn't matter, took no notice.

Her marriage to a dull dog of a Dane called George was happy, but hard work. Between 1685 and 1700 she was pregnant eighteen times; yet, sad to say, she died without heir.

After her quarrel with the Duchess of Marlborough she had to try to govern the country on her own, but it wasn't easy. Opportunism and intrigue among ministers and the clergy were a handicap, and she herself was not what you would call one of the brightest. She preferred the company of politicians and parsons to that of poets and painters, having a horror of the arts that endeared her warmly to her people. Their affection for her was deepened by her love of horseflesh and to this day her name is revered at Ladbroke's, as well as by Joe Corral, Jack Solomons and Terry Downes, as the founder of the Ascot meeting. Despite this, there is no doubt that life at Queen Anne's court was dull. But it did have one thing to recommend it: Lord Chesterfield disapproved of it.

GEORGE I
1714-1727

As King of England, George I laboured under a number of disadvantages. Number 1, he was a German, and Number 2, he could speak no English. Nor did it help matters that none of his ministers could speak a word of German. Such direct communication as there was between them was therefore conducted in dumb show, with results that were sometimes amusing and occasionally *risqué* when a word or a gesture was misunderstood. However, as the King loathed England and spent as much time as possible in Germany, the need for consultation with his ministers didn't often arise. He did manage to make himself understood, however, when he needed English money with which to stuff the pockets of his German favourites, or to supply the wants of a string of great fat German mistresses; otherwise he left England to stew in its own juice, for which England was profoundly grateful.

GEORGE II
1727-1760

George II was no better than his horrible old *vater*. In fact, he was worse, because he preferred to live in England rather than Germany. He was just as quarrelsome and stupid as the old man and hadn't a clue about major matters of policy, but was red hot over petty details, such as the execution of Admiral Byng for dereliction of duty. This was rather odd, as a matter of fact, because the populace wanted the admiral's blood too, and usually it only had to be said that George approved of something for the populace to shout it down.

Being a German, George couldn't keep his nose out of politics, but complained when Pitt was PM that he couldn't understand a word of what he was talking about. It must be admitted, however, that this may not have been George's fault.

In his favour it should be added that he fostered the talents of George Frederick Handel, thereby incurring the derision of the British aristocracy.

GEORGE III
1760-1820

After Georges I and II, George III was greeted on his accession with marked reserve. The thought of another Hanoverian monstrosity on the throne of England was too much. As E. C. Bentley remarked:

> George the Third
> Ought never to have occurred.
> One can only wonder
> At so grotesque a blunder.

Nevertheless, the public's fears were to some extent dispelled by the new king's first speech to Parliament, in which he declared: 'Bourn end bredt in zis guntry, I clory in zer naeme off Bridon.' By this well-chosen utterance George established for himself a fund of goodwill that lasted for at least ten days.

He soon made it clear that in politics he was by no means the dolt his grandfather, George II had been, nor such an imbecile, and those who blamed him at the time for the loss of the American colonies would no doubt have praised him for the same reason if they could have foreseen what they were going to turn into.

As is well known, George III suffered from bouts of insanity. (It is odd, incidentally, that similar attacks in earlier kings have usually been accepted as part of their normal behaviour.) On one such occasion he scared the daylights out of Fanny Burney by chasing her round Kew Gardens. Not that this was necessarily a sign of madness. She was, as a matter of fact, an attractive gel and had I been a blade in 1789 I might have done the same. But George was hardly a blade, or if so, rather a blunt one, being at that time over fifty.

It is generally believed that George III was the first British sovereign since Canute to go in for sea bathing. This he used to do at Weymouth from a bathing machine, climbing backwards down the steps while the band of the Grenadier Guards, submerged to the waist, played 'God Save the King'.

If his somewhat limited conception of the monarchy's role in public affairs made him, as time progressed, none too popular, it is pleasant to think that his insanity brought with it a renewal of fellow-feeling between him and his subjects.

GEORGE IV
1820-1830

George IV began life under the handicap of being a son of
George III. Added to this were a natural tendency towards loose
living, coupled with the instincts of a cad, and in due course the
bulk of a hippopotamus. Though he was not the only King of
England who was a bigamist, he was probably the only one who
wore stays. He also kept mistresses and got stoned every night.
On one occasion he also got stoned during the day while on his
way to open Parliament. In this way the populace indicated what
they thought of him, and on the whole it may be said that posterity
seems to think the same.

WILLIAM IV
1830-1837

I've nothing against William IV personally, but honestly, he was half-saved. Known as Pineapple Poll, because of the shape of his head, his sun-burnt countenance, and the texture of his facial epidermis, he was by rights just a bluff sailor. Unfortunately, he didn't confine his bluffing to nautical affairs and when he tried, as frequently he did, to interfere in politics, he usually ran aground.

For twenty years he lived happily in sin with the charming actress, Mrs Jordan. Then his niece, Princess Charlotte, who was next in line to the throne, died, leaving him without obstruction in front of the hoop. The stern call of duty sounding in his ear, he jettisoned Jordan in order to marry and beget himself an heir. Though he and his queen, Adelaide of Saxe-Meiningen, strove with commendable persistence to bring this about, their efforts were of no avail. Childless to the last, William died on 20 June 1837.

VICTORIA
1837-1901

The circumstances in which Queen Victoria came to the throne are rather unusual. To start with it was in the middle of the night, and furthermore she was under the age of consent. Nevertheless, she consented immediately, her tender years preventing a realization of the trials and tribulations she was letting herself in for (e.g. Mr Gladstone, Dean Stanley, etc.).

How it was that she was there when the call came is a sad and somewhat sordid story. The King, her uncle, had no children and his predecessor, George IV, had had but one child, Princess Charlotte, who had died in 1817. Though George was only forty-five, the chances of his fathering another legitimate heir seemed, all things considered, remote. He and his wife, Carrie Brunswick, hadn't been on speaking terms for years, and in 1821 she died. So there he was, childless, fat as a pig, and steeped in vice, and, with such a figure and such habits, unlikely to marry again. As soon as the implications of this sank into the minds of his brothers – and the percolation of all but the most elementary ideas was a slow process – three of them dashed off and with unseemly haste strove to plug the gap left by Princess Charlotte's death; the fourth brother, Augustus, Duke of Sussex, couldn't even find a wife.

First past the post was Edward, Duke of Kent, who had taken as his spouse a woman as dull and undistinguished as himself, Princess Victoria of Saxe-Coburg, from whose inauspicious loins sprang the great Queen whose reign is commemorated by a railway terminus, an embankment, a coach station, and inumerable pubs.

It is said that on being told by her governess, Baroness Lehzen, that one day she would become queen, the little princess remarked, 'I will be good.' A misconception has arisen about this incident. In fact, what the princess actually said was, 'I will be? Good!'

The young Queen, though well brought up, was of a passionate nature; a contradiction in terms that was bound to lead to difficulties. All her life she felt a deep need for male support, and when she was temporarily deprived of it or felt disinclined to trust her weight to it, all was gloom. The first to lend a reassuring arm was good old, kind old, cynical old Lord Melbourne. When the cruel exigencies of politics deprived her of his support, she

leant gingerly on the arm of Sir Robert Peel, and then recoiled. The mainstay of her life, of course, was Albert the Bore. This pious, beefy, solemn, industrious Teuton supplied her with some obscure but deep-seated need and it vexed the Queen that she seemed to be the only one who appreciated it. Her marriage with Albert was an idyllic union, though it did not seem so to Edward, Prince of Wales, on whom both parents lavished disapproval and discouragement as others lavish love upon their first-born son.

After Albert's departure for Valhalla via Windsor in 1861, came the Queen's long withdrawal into the vale of tears and temperamental tantrums, from which she was gradually enticed by the magical charms of Dizzy the Dandy. By what means this brilliant but unctuous creep steered her from her twilit cavern of gloom back into the light of popular esteem no one can say. That he did so is a testimony to his diplomatic skill and psychological insight.

And then, of course, there was John Brown. The power exercised over the Queen by this gruff and insufferable ghillie is even more mysterious than that exercised by Disraeli. Brown was permitted liberties with the royal person, as in the handing of it into or out of a carriage or mounting it upon a Highland pony, that would have earned a less favoured menial a thwack from the royal parasol.

By the time the Queen shuffled off this mortal coil to join Albert the Bore elsewhere in an eternal embrace, the wheel had come full circle. The dreary interval of her long hibernation was forgotten and forgiven. The affection that had been felt for the promising and high-spirited novice was re-aroused by the fat and venerable 'fairy' of Disraeli's shallow compliment. It was no mean feat on the Queen's part to rescue the monarchy from the ditch where it had been left by the Georges, and by George, she did it!

Victoria's reign saw immense changes in both the political and social climate. Reform, Chartism, the Oxford Movement (easy to perform – a step to the Right, down on your knees, bow your head, now twitch the nostrils: if you can smell incense you're home and dry). Then there was the railway boom, a rude noise made by George Hudson, leading light of the *nouveaux riches*, at whose name ladies of gentle breeding were inclined to feel faint. From abroad in 1848 came ruder noises, the steady tramp of Garibaldi's bunioned *banditti* the embarrassing gurgle of democratic juices at work in the body politic. There was Expo 1851. There was the Crimean War and the crinoline, each equally inessential. Then there was the bicycle and the bustle, of which the former was the more comfortable to ride on. There was Church Parade and there was the Royal Academy – like the poor, always with us and much to be pitied. There was Gilbert and Sullivan, Huntley and Palmer, Whistler and Wilde (ssh, dear!). There was Bradlaugh and Besant, the comedy duo of the new free-thinking, free-loving society. And above all, pinnacled on the affection of her peoples, was the stumpy, dumpy, grumpy old Widow of Windsor, *Victoria Imperatrix.*

EDWARD VII
1901-1910

As a youth Edward was a deep disappointment to his parents, being in every way a normal lad. After the death of his Papa, his Mama, knowing that Albert would have wished it, continued to disapprove. Her refusal to entrust Edward with even the most insignificant responsibilities of state threw him much upon his own resources; among these were Nellie Clifden, Lady Brooke, Mrs George Keppel, Lily Langtry, etc., etc., etc. He also took an ardent interest in his clothes and will probably be best remembered for helping to popularize the wing-collar, the Homburg hat, and the spat.

The Queen's disapprobation notwithstanding, Edward was a favourite with the *hoi polloi*, which saw in him a character with instincts and appetites as commonplace as its own.

In the days of his great-uncle George, Edward would have been known as a rattle. He enjoyed the company of ladies, was fond of racing, gambling and high living, and wore his hat on one side. Because of his dashing personality he was known as Edward the Pacemaker. He had an exquisite sense of humour, as was shown at a dinner party when he poured a bottle of brandy over the head of a guest. But he knew where to draw the line and thought it not at all funny when Lily Langtry slipped a lemon sorbet down the back of his neck.

Edward was an inveterate smoker of cigars and also had a fondness for Danish pastries, one of whom he married: the beautiful Princess Alexandra of Schleswig-Holstein-Sonderburg-Glucksburg and change at Rumpenheim for Frankfurt.

The reign of King Edward was on the whole uneventful except for one major catastrophe: improvements were made in the internal combustion engine.

GEORGE V
1910-1936

George V was affectionately known as Our Sailor King because of his fondness for wearing a yachting cap. He is considered on the whole to have been a good king and his faults seem to have been few and far between. It was not his fault, for instance, that he was half the size of Queen Mary: it was just one of those things. At the same time, he does seem to have had two rather serious faults: he wore *black socks* with plimsolls, and was given to bad language. This might, however, be excused on the ground that there were provocations, among them Mr Asquith, the German Emperor, the Irish Question, and the suffragettes, who were enough to make anybody swear – earnest and vociferous females, their clothes hopelessly unfashionable, and their behaviour aggressive, their favourite trick was to chain themselves to railings and throw away the key. Half-baked notions of humanitarianism caused the Home Secretary to order that they should be unchained. A great mistake.

In 1911 King George went to Delhi with the Queen for a tremendous shenannigans, which translated from the Erse means Durbar. All the Indian princes turned up, gorgeously arrayed, as was George, in his coronation robes of imperial purple, his mantelet of miniver, his tunic of cloth of gold, and his yachting cap. If the Durbar was one of the high-spots of George's reign, another was the First World War, in which he went about in the undress uniform of a field-marshal, armed with a walking stick. He did a good job encouraging everybody and pretending not to mind, and was actually wounded, though not by the Germans; it was by his own horse, which shied on catching sight of Sir Douglas Haig, fell over backward and rolled on top of the King. But he survived, and so, alas, did Sir Douglas Haig.

Not much happened after that, except the General Strike of 1926, when the King went bravely on with his stamp collection, ignoring the sound of tumbrils in the Mall. Stamps were not his only interest, though very nearly. He was also a crack shot and at sixty yards could pick a stuffed humming bird off Queen Mary's toque. As king, George's achievements, like his own demeanour, were modest, his most worthy being no doubt the example he set of doing a boring job conscientiously and with good humour.

His dying words are well known: 'What's on at the Empire?'

QUEEN MARY
1910-1936

Queen Mary, though never regnant, was every inch (62-58-60) a queen, and so is here treated as such.

Victoria Mary Augusta Louise Olga Pauline Claudine Agnes, as she was called for short, had a passion for antiques, attested to by a life-long devotion to George V. Princess May, as she then was, achieved royal status as the result of a strange accident of fate known as Albert, Duke of Clarence, the eldest son of Edward VII.

It would be wrong to say that Clarence failed at everything he tried his hand at because the only thing he tried it at was chemmy, and he often won. In due course it was announced that Clarence was engaged to Princess May, and then, with lack a of persistence that had for long troubled his parents, he excelled himself by dying. But by a stroke of good luck a substitute was conveniently at hand – Clarence's younger brother, George, dutiful, upright and clean-limbed (as far as one could tell – he creased his trousers down the side). On 3 July 1893, he and May were married and lived happily ever after.

During the First World War Queen Mary was deeply interested in relief work, dispensing bismuth tablets to wounded soldiers, standing up for the nursing profession, lying down for forty winks, opening bazaars, closing ranks, and generally putting her not inconsiderable shoulder to the wheel. Though she will long be remembered for her indefatigable sense of public duty, there is, as yet, no statue of her. This seems rather unfair, seeing that she was, above all, statuesque, and that London's pigeons are short of statues. It is to be hoped that in the not too distant future Henry Moore will be invited to have a go.

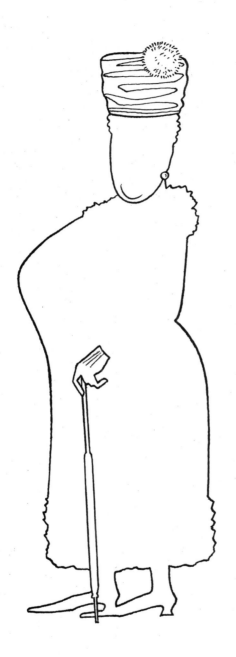

EDWARD VIII
-1936-

As Prince of Wales, Edward VIII endeared himself to the populace by being a fearless rider to hounds and an equally fearless faller-off. He also had a beaming smile and radiated an infectious gaiety. Some, however, were immune from its infection, among them the Prime Minister, Stanley Baldwin, who never forgave the prince for suggesting that somebody should do something about the living conditions of the unemployed.

However, Baldwin got his own back later on. The prince had become enamoured of an American lady called Mrs Ernest Simpson. Now, the trouble was not only Mr Ernest Simpson, but also a Mr Earl Winfield Spencer, Jnr, to whom Mrs Simpson had been wed at an earlier date, and had since divorced. The importance of being Ernest was never more clearly demonstrated than when Mrs Simpson found she wanted to marry the King, as the prince had now become. This she could not do while Ernest remained as an impediment. Then by a strange and happy coincidence grounds were discovered for divorcing him. Well, Mr Baldwin, who was exceptionally short-sighted about the state of the country in most respects, thought he could see one thing quite clearly: the country would never stand for a queen who was a divorcée twice over and an American to boot; and the constitution wouldn't stand for the King making a morganatic marriage. So there the PM sat, puffing away at his pipe and chuckling with his pal the archbishop, known as 'Cant' Lang.

For once in his life Mr Baldwin may have been right. No one will ever know because the King abdicated, thereby endearing himself to the populace all over again by sacrificing all for love. Everybody was very sorry and some thought the King had had a raw deal. But many felt somehow that patriotic, pipe-puffing old Stanley could always be trusted to do the right thing. They had to wait till 1939 to find out that he'd done damn all about the things that mattered most.

GEORGE VI
1936-1952

George VI, whose name was Albert, didn't have much of an innings, through no fault of his own. Being only a reserve, he didn't expect to have to leave the pavilion, but when called upon, he put up a jolly good show.

Before going in to bat, he used to have to go to boys' camps, wearing shorts, and join in the community singing (with actions). The appearance that he managed to sustain of actually enjoying himself on these occasions endeared him to one and all. Definitely a good king.

ELIZABETH II
1952-

Our own Queen, Elizabeth II, succeeded on 6 February 1952, proving once again the old adage that nothing succeeds like succeeding.

Queen Elizabeth is beloved of her people and beloves them in return. Some are sufficiently well-beloved to be invited to luncheon at Buckingham Palace, where they may quite possibly find themselves sitting next to a novelist, a race-horse trainer, a trade union leader, or worse, a Fellow of the Royal Society. But this is a democratic age and they have to lump it.

The Queen loves not only her people; she also loves corgis; and she loves the Badminton Horse Trials, the Richmond Horse Show, the White City Show-Jumping Championships, the Derby, the Oaks, the Lincoln, the Gold Cup, the Hunt Cup, the Windsor Selling Plate, etc.

She is the first truly democratic queen we have ever had and does a grand job, honestly, holding together the bonds of the Commonwealth whence all but she have fled, and mingling freely with the common people, such as the Duke of Norfolk, the Duke of Beaufort, Earl Mountbatten, the Countess of Euston, the Lady Margaret Hay, Lieutenant-Colonel the Right Hon. Sir Michael Adeane, Sir Anthony Wagner, Garter King of Arms, and others whom you might see any day of the week tooling along Oxford Street or Deansgate, Manchester.

In 1947 the Queen married Prince Philip (affectionately known as My Husband and I), until then a practically unknown quantity, but vaguely thought to be some sort of Greek. Her coronation in Westminster Abbey on 2 June 1953 was a scene of magnificence unparalleled even by Selfridge's Christmas decorations.

Not least among the acts for which the Queen will go down in history, and up in posterity's estimation, is her single-handed attempt at suppression of the Debs. The species, however, is tenacious of existence and pockets are still said to exist among tribes that dwell in the hinterlands of Belgravia and Chelsea.

It is widely believed, because it is just the kind of thing that *Daily Express* and *Woman's Realm* readers like widely to believe, that the Queen, no less than the more obvious possibility of her husband, was influential in the decision to submit their first-born, bonny Prince Charley the second, to the rigours first of Gordons-

toun, that nursery of independence, hardihood, bruised kneecaps and chattering teeth, then to push him Down Under, and if he came up (smiling), which as luck would have it, he did, to let him recuperate under the watchful, benevolent, slightly lop-sided smile, if you can call it that, of Lord Butler. And if ever a man had cause for a lop-sided smile, it is Lord Butler.

Neither the Queen, nor Prince Philip, or probably Lord Butler, let alone you or I, could have foreseen that in spite of Gordonstoun, in *spite* of Down Under, in SPITE of a family tradition of more than a hundred years of almost total indifference to the arts, bonny Prince Charley would take to playing the cello. It is said that when news of this catastrophe reached Buckingham Palace, the shaking of heads and shrugging of shoulders was such that the Brazilian Ambassador, at that moment entering upon an audience with the Queen, and believing that the hokey-cokey was in progress, ventured to join in.

The Queen, as we know, is a good and loving Momma. Her reign amply proves, to those who may feel sceptical, that it is possible to combine the role of wife and mother with that of a constitutional monarch, providing you've got the constitution. Though troubles may beset the creaking timbers of the ship of state, though the pound may be devalued (again), there is little likelihood that the value of the sovereign, so long as it happens to be Queen Elizabeth the Second, will ever fall below par.

GOD SAVE THE QUEEN